Crabapples

What Do You See Under the Sea?

Bobbie Kalman

Diving photographs by Christopher Hartley

Crabtree Publishing Company

Crabapples

created by Bobbie Kalman

For Christopher and Yuri Hartley

Editor-in-Chief
Bobbie Kalman

Managing editor
Lynda Hale

Editors
Petrina Gentile
Tammy Everts
Niki Walker
Greg Nickles

Computer design
Lynda Hale

Costume coordinator
Janine Schaub

Color separations and film
Dot 'n Line Image Inc.

Printer
Worzalla Publishing Company

Illustrations
Barb Bedell
Tammy Everts: page 32

Special thanks to
Nicola and Sascha Hill, Nicholas Stanko, Kelly Ferguson, and
Cliffeen McPhee

**All undersea walk photographs were taken by, or are the property
of, Christopher Hartley:** cover, title page, pages 4, 5 (both), 6,
8 (top), 9 (top), 10, 12, 14 (top), 15 (top), 16 (both), 17, 18 (both),
20, 22 (top), 23 (top), 24 (top), 25 (top), 26 (top), 27 (both), 28, 32

Other photographs
Bob Cranston: page 26 (bottom)
Cindy Garoutte/Tom Stack & Associates: page 7
David Gilchrist: page 9 (bottom)
Lynda Hale: page 3 (bottom)
Paul H. Humann: pages 25 (bottom), 29
Paul L. Janosi: pages 13, 23 (bottom)
Bobbie Kalman: pages 15 (bottom), 22 (bottom)
Linda Menzies: page 24 (bottom)
Brian Parker/Tom Stack & Associates: page 21
David Sailors: pages 8 (bottom), 11, 12 (bottom)
David Schimpky: page 3 (top)

For more information, contact Hartley's Undersea Walk,
Nassau Yacht Haven, Bahamas, (809) 393-8234

Crabtree Publishing Company

350 Fifth Avenue
Suite 3308
New York
N.Y. 10118

360 York Road, RR 4,
Niagara-on-the-Lake,
Ontario, Canada
L0S 1J0

73 Lime Walk
Headington
Oxford OX3 7AD
United Kingdom

Cataloging in Publication Data
Kalman, Bobbie, 1947-
    What do you see under the sea?

(Crabapples)
Includes index.

ISBN 0-86505-621-8 (library bound)   ISBN 0-86505-721-4 (pbk.)
Ocean creatures are introduced in an undersea walk that
is full of surprises!

1. Marine biology - Juvenile literature. I. Title. II. Series:
Kalman, Bobbie, 1947-   . Crabapples.

QH91.16.K35 1995   j574.92   LC 95-36477
                                                  CIP

We are going on an undersea walk. We travel by boat to a **coral reef** in the ocean near Nassau, Bahamas. We put on diving helmets. Air is pumped into our helmets through hoses. Can you see them in the water? We keep our knees bent and walk carefully. We do not want to kick up sand on the ocean floor.

Christopher Hartley is our photographer and guide. He shows us the amazing creatures that live in the reef. His kitten wonders why she is the one in the bowl instead of Harry the Nassau grouper.

When we arrive at the reef, Harry comes to greet us. Chris has trained Harry to allow visitors to hold and pet him.

In case Harry is eaten by a bigger fish, Chris has also trained two junior groupers to take Harry's place. The junior groupers stay away from Harry. Harry is definitely the boss!

Harry invites you to join us. We have planned some surprises for you! What do you think you will see under the sea?

What do you see under the sea?

A small teddy bear…

and a great barracuda. A barracuda has
many sharp teeth. It eats other fish.

What do you see under the sea?

A cucumber that is a vegetable…

and a sea cucumber, which is an animal. Sea cucumbers live in shallow sandy areas near coral reefs. They move very slowly on the ocean floor.

8

What do you see under the sea?

A baseball fan…

and a sea fan. A sea fan is
a coral with tiny branches.
Sea fans can be yellow,
pink, brown, or purple.

What do you see under the sea?

A girl playing a trumpet...

Blow, Harry, blow!

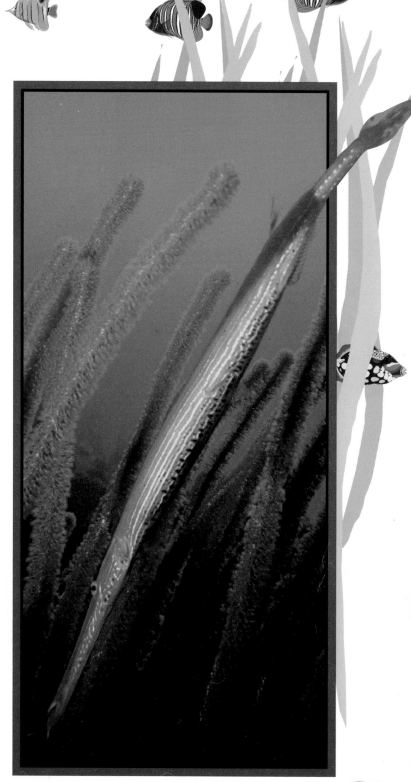

and a trumpetfish.
This trumpetfish
is hiding from its
enemies. It blends in
well with the sea rods
around it. Does a
trumpetfish blow
its own horn?

What do you see under the sea?

Three beautiful butterflies…

and a foureye butterflyfish.
Foureye butterflyfish have two
false eyes near their tail.

What does she see under the sea?

Does she see
a sea enemy…

or does she see a sea
anemone? This giant
anemone may look
like a flower, but it
can kill fish with its
stinging tentacles!

What do you see under the sea?

A surgeon taking
a patient's pulse…

Harry M.D.

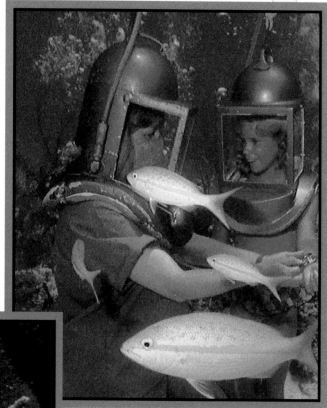

and a surgeonfish.
A surgeonfish has
a spine that is as
sharp as a scalpel on
both sides of its tail.
Would you let this
ocean surgeonfish
take out your tonsils?

What do you see under the sea?

A Christmas tree
trimmed with red bows…

and two red Christmas tree worms.
Christmas tree worms quickly pull
their tentacles back into their tube
when something frightens them.

What do you see under the sea?

Some fingers…

18

and some finger coral. Finger coral looks fuzzy
when it is awake and smooth when it is asleep.

What do you see under the sea?

A diver in a sergeant major uniform…

20

and a school of sergeant major
fish swimming around a diver.

What do you see under the sea?

A movie star, Harry the star…

and a sea star. If a sea star's arm breaks off, another one grows in its place.

What do you see under the sea?

Drummers in spots...

and a fish called a spotted drum. This fish makes a noise that sounds like someone playing a drum.

23

What do you see under the sea?

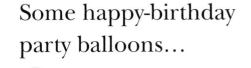

Some happy-birthday party balloons…

and an angry balloonfish. Balloonfish fill themselves with water and poke out their spines when something disturbs them.

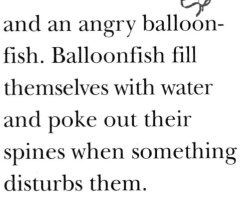

What do you see under the sea?

A peppermint candy cane…

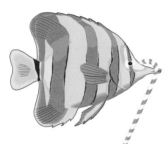

and a peppermint bass. During the day, this small fish hides in undersea caves.

What do you see under the sea?

A man of peace…

and a Portuguese man-of-war. Don't tangle with this jellyfish's long tentacles. They really sting!

What do you see under the sea?

A boy doing
hoop tricks…

and a queen
angelfish doing
hoop tricks.
Angelfish are
graceful swimmers.

27

What do you see under the sea?

A clown entertaining a school of fish...

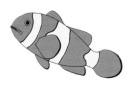

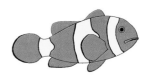

and a clown wrasse. Clown wrasses live in the Caribbean Sea and the Atlantic Ocean near Florida. The orange fish are clown fish. They live in the Pacific and Indian oceans.

Picture glossary & index

anemone (giant sea anemone)
page 14

angelfish
page 27

balloonfish
page 24

barracuda
page 7

Christmas tree worm
page 17

butterflyfish
page 13

clown wrasse
page 29

clown fish
page 29

coral reef
pages 3, 4, 5, 8

finger coral
page 19

Harry the
**Nassau
grouper**
pages 4, 5, 11,
15, 16, 22, 23,
26, 29

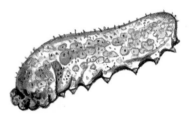

peppermint bass
page 25

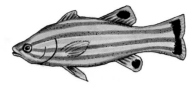

Portuguese man-of-war
page 26

sea cucumber
page 8

sea fan
page 9

sea star
page 22

sergeant major
page 21

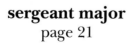

spotted drum
page 23

surgeonfish
page 15

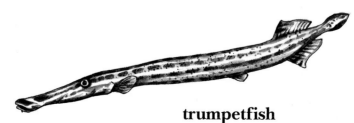

trumpetfish
page 11

Chris Hartley's walk

Christopher Hartley was born in Bermuda and has lived in the United States, Canada, and Switzerland. He now lives in Nassau, Bahamas. Chris spends much of his time in the ocean. He began diving at the age of a year and a day. In January 1995, he and his wife Yuri were married under the sea!

On Chris's undersea walks, you can learn firsthand about ocean life, even if you cannot swim. The heavy diving helmet keeps you down on the ocean floor. It allows you to breathe normally underwater. The walk is amazing!

air hose

diving helmet